MAJESTIC OCEANS

Discover The World Beneath the Waves

ORANGE
M·O·S·Q·U·I·T·O

MIA CASSANY · MARCOS NAVARRO

MAP OF THE

SOME 70% OF OUR PLANET IS COVERED BY THE SEAS AND OCEANS.

ANTARCTICA'S ICE IS OUR LARGEST FRESH WATER RESERVE: IT HOLDS AROUND 81% OF THE WORLD'S DRINKABLE WATER.

ARCTIC OCEAN

RØST

AZORES

GIANT KELP FOREST

GULF OF CALIFORNIA

NORTH ATLANTIC OCEAN

NORTH PACIFIC OCEAN

CAPE VERD

COCOS ISLAND

SOUTH ATLANTIC OCEA

FLYING FISH

SOUTH PACIFIC OCEAN

FALKLAND ISLANDS

SOUTHERN OCEA

For Maddi, my family and friends. And especially
for all young nature lovers. MARCOS
MARCOS

Lluís, Inma, Joan Marc and Antoine, always.
MIA

After drawing jungles and rainforests © Marcos Navarro was
ready to dive in and illustrate the wonders that hide beneath the
waves. © Mia Cassany really wanted to tell you everything about
our oceans and how to protect them. Because oceans are life.

Published in 2022 by Orange Mosquito
An Imprint of Welbeck Children's Limited
part of Welbeck Publishing Group.
Based in London and Sydney.
www.welbeckpublishing.com

In collaboration with Mosquito Books Barcelona S.L.

© Mosquito Books Barcelona, SL 2022
Text © Mia Cassany 2022
Illustration © Marcos Navarro 2022
Translation: Clare Gaunt
Publisher: Margaux Durigon
Production: Jess Brisley

ISBN: 9781914519321
eISBN: 9781914519338

Printed in China
10 9 8 7 6 5 4 3 2 1

WORLD'S OCEANS

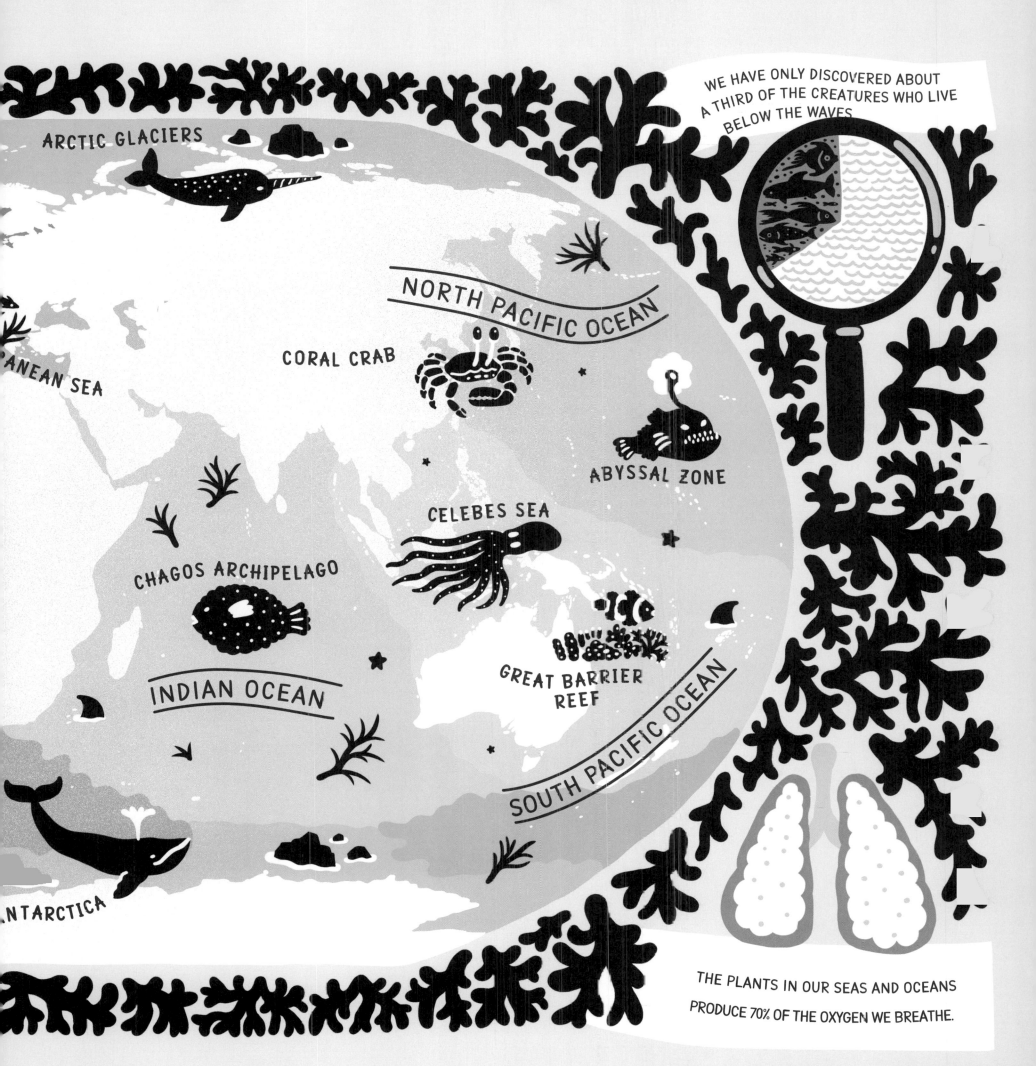

ARCTIC GLACIERS

...ANEAN SEA

CORAL CRAB

NORTH PACIFIC OCEAN

ABYSSAL ZONE

CELEBES SEA

CHAGOS ARCHIPELAGO

INDIAN OCEAN

GREAT BARRIER REEF

SOUTH PACIFIC OCEAN

...NTARCTICA

WE HAVE ONLY DISCOVERED ABOUT A THIRD OF THE CREATURES WHO LIVE BELOW THE WAVES

THE PLANTS IN OUR SEAS AND OCEANS PRODUCE 70% OF THE OXYGEN WE BREATHE.

GIANT KELP FOREST

In the Pacific Ocean, off the west coast of North America in the state of California, lies an incredibly important National Park formed by eight fabulous islands.

This protected area is a UNESCO Biosphere Reserve.

Here, the island waters are home to over 30 species of giant seaweed which form the largest underwater forests on the planet. These giant algae are a habitat, hiding place, safe zone, and rich source of food for numerous ocean creatures. And although it may seem hard to believe, kelp doesn't belong to the green algae family, it is actually a protist. (A protist is a group of living things with one cell and which are not animals, plants, fungi, or bacteria.)

As you can see, these dense kelp forests are one of the planet's most beautiful aquatic environments.

ARCTIC OCEAN

The Arctic Ocean is also known as the Arctic Mediterranean Sea because it is the smallest of the earth's oceans. It lies to the north of the Arctic Circle.

This is our coldest ocean and it is covered in layers of sea ice. Very low temperatures and extreme conditions make it a tough environment, but for some animals, it is the perfect home.

For centuries, it has been home to seals, although their numbers have declined significantly in recent years; due to hunting and the melting ice caps caused particularly by global warming.

It is also home to some of the world's largest, most magnificent animals: orcas and whales. But they too are suffering from the "great thaw."

The Arctic is a great place to spot giant tusked walruses, the massive beluga whale, and its relative, the narwhal.

SEARCH & FIND
19
ANIMALS!

THE GREAT BARRIER REEF

You'll find the world's largest coral reef to the northeast of Australia, just off the coast of Queensland.

This huge colony of hard corals can only survive in the ocean. When coral dies, its beautiful, tough skeleton remains on the sea bed, forming the foundation for new colonies of magnificent corals.

Many biologists see the Great Barrier Reef as the planet's largest living being—it extends across thousands of miles. Declared a UNESCO World Heritage Site, it is home to one of the largest concentrations of biodiversity in the marine world.

Coral is very sensitive to temperature change, and the reef is already suffering badly from global warming.

Some of the other marine species in these beautiful waters include the dugong (a marine mammal), massive green sea turtles, and snappers.

SEARCH & FIND
29
ANIMALS!

SOUTHERN OCEAN

The Southern Ocean goes all the way around Antarctica.

It is the world's second smallest ocean, measuring only 7.7 million square miles. Only the Arctic Ocean is smaller.

The Southern Ocean is a vital ecosystem. Huge, magnificent whales have swum around the South Pole for thousands of years. They migrate here in summer to fatten up on krill as Antarctica is home to one of the world's biggest krill populations. The tiny crustacean is an important food source for all kinds of sea creatures, including baleen whales, squid, and penguins! Without krill, our greatest cetaceans (whales) would simply disappear.

Many countries (including the United Kingdom, the United States, Australia, France, Japan, and South Africa) signed the Antarctic Treaty to protect the Southern Ocean's spectacular marine flora and fauna from human encroachment. All of the signatories promise to take care of this part of the world, for future generations to enjoy: we have to conserve this unique marine environment.

SEARCH & FIND
3
ANIMALS!

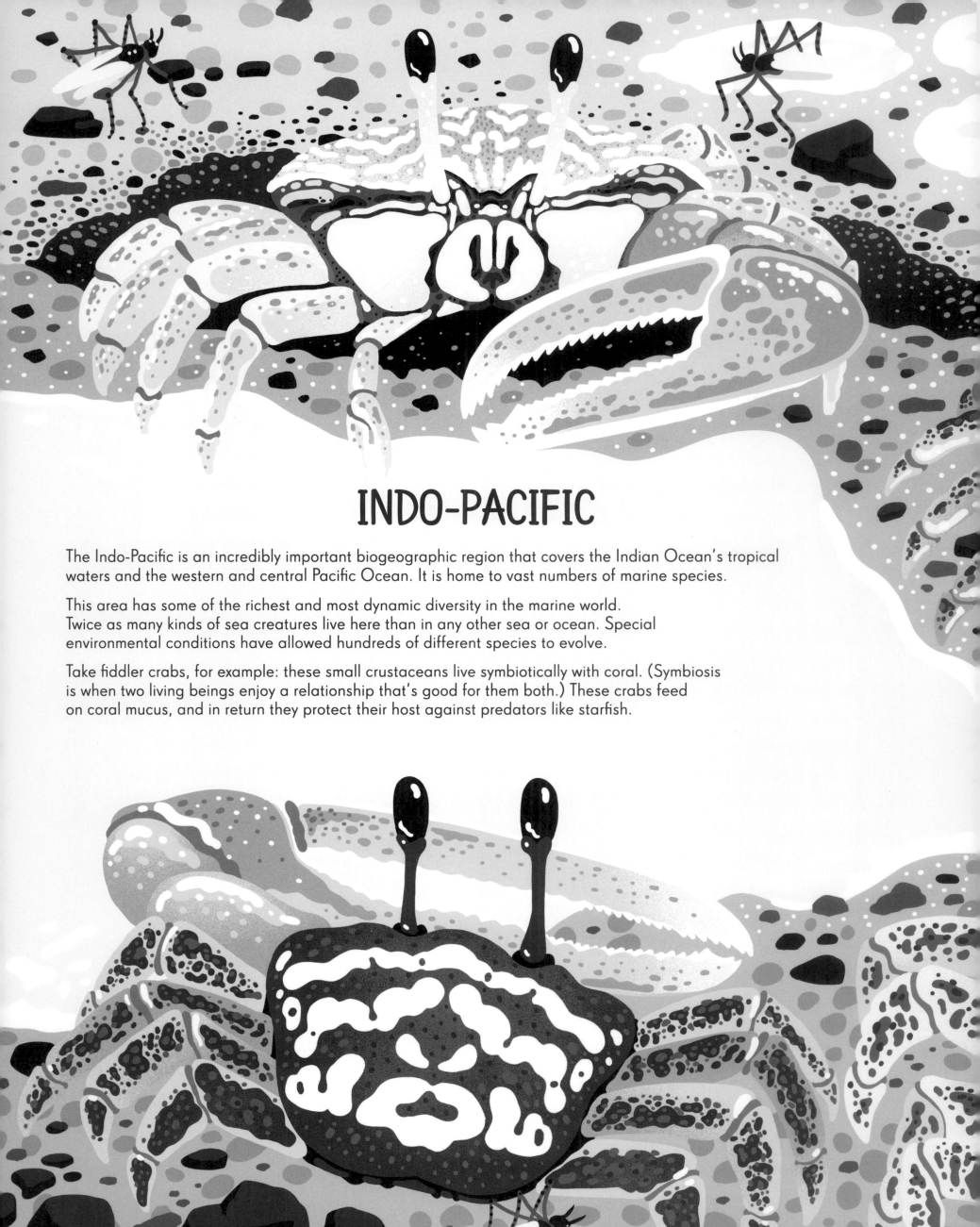

INDO-PACIFIC

The Indo-Pacific is an incredibly important biogeographic region that covers the Indian Ocean's tropical waters and the western and central Pacific Ocean. It is home to vast numbers of marine species.

This area has some of the richest and most dynamic diversity in the marine world. Twice as many kinds of sea creatures live here than in any other sea or ocean. Special environmental conditions have allowed hundreds of different species to evolve.

Take fiddler crabs, for example: these small crustaceans live symbiotically with coral. (Symbiosis is when two living beings enjoy a relationship that's good for them both.) These crabs feed on coral mucus, and in return they protect their host against predators like starfish.

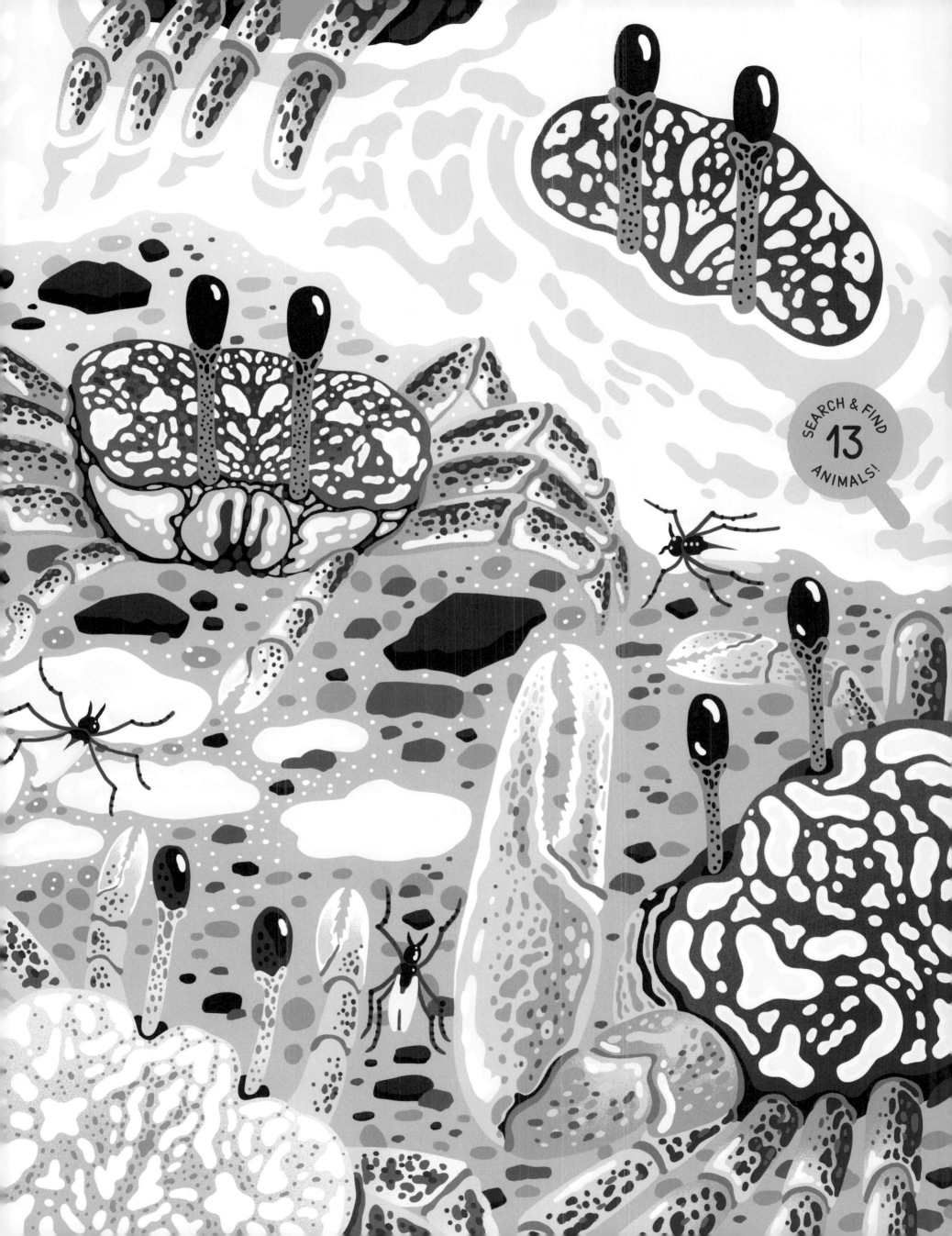

SEARCH & FIND
13
ANIMALS!

COCOS ISLAND

Cocos Island sits in the middle of the Pacific Ocean. It is part of the Central American Republic of Costa Rica.

The entire volcanic island is a National Park.

Only a few lucky biologists and marine researchers are allowed to stay on this isolated and uninhabited island. Its unique features make it the perfect laboratory to study the remarkable species that live here and find out how they have evolved. We're lucky to have such a special place on our planet.

The species that live here have evolved free of outside influence. Several types of shark swim in the island waters, including: whale sharks, huge shoals of hammerheads, and tiger sharks.

Cocos island is also home to yellowfin tuna and critically endangered hawksbill sea turtles.

SEARCH & FIND
60
ANIMALS!

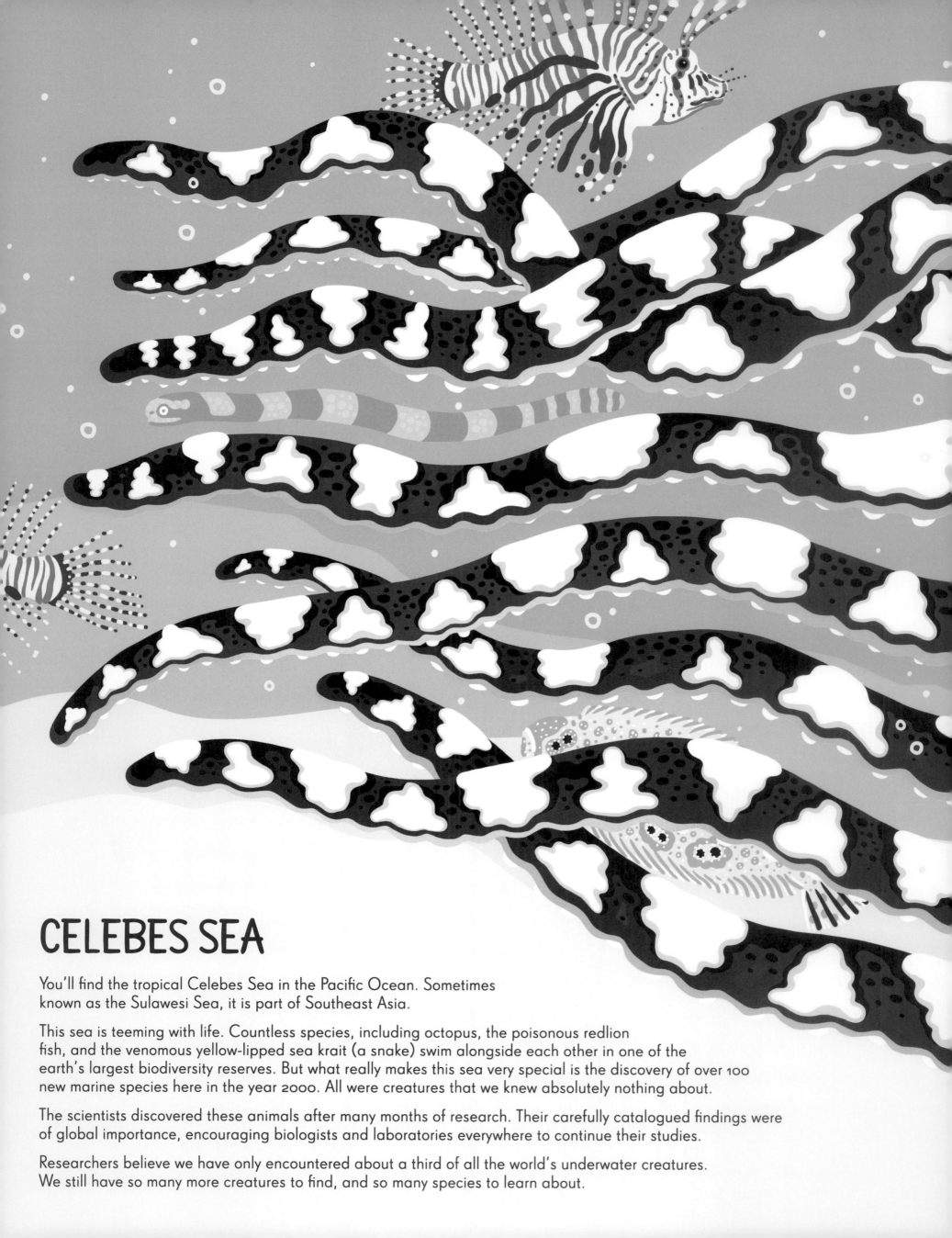

CELEBES SEA

You'll find the tropical Celebes Sea in the Pacific Ocean. Sometimes known as the Sulawesi Sea, it is part of Southeast Asia.

This sea is teeming with life. Countless species, including octopus, the poisonous redlion fish, and the venomous yellow-lipped sea krait (a snake) swim alongside each other in one of the earth's largest biodiversity reserves. But what really makes this sea very special is the discovery of over 100 new marine species here in the year 2000. All were creatures that we knew absolutely nothing about.

The scientists discovered these animals after many months of research. Their carefully catalogued findings were of global importance, encouraging biologists and laboratories everywhere to continue their studies.

Researchers believe we have only encountered about a third of all the world's underwater creatures. We still have so many more creatures to find, and so many species to learn about.

SEARCH & FIND
8
ANIMALS!

RØST REEF, THE LOFOTEN ISLANDS

One of the world's most remarkable deep sea locations is found in an area of the Atlantic Ocean more commonly known as the Nordic Seas.

The coastal areas of Norway's Lofoten islands are home to the Røst Reef. The largest deep water reef we have ever discovered is similar to the Great Barrier Reef; but it is formed of cold-water corals. These corals are home to all kinds of spectacular creatures, from plankton, to fish like the conger eel, blackbelly rosefish, angler fish, plus jellyfish and lobsters.

One of the things that makes this place so special is that we hardly know anything about it. Only a tiny portion of these murky depths have been explored.

Deep-sea exploration is tricky as there is no sunlight, making it harder to see things. Nevertheless scientists and marine biologists are constantly working to find out more about our hidden world.

CAPE VERDE

The volcanic archipelago of Cape Verde lies off the coast of Africa, in the Atlantic Ocean. It is made up of five large and five smaller islands. Being far away from big cities and trade routes has protected it from pollution.

Over 17 different species of whales and dolphins swim through these waters. Dolphins are one of the world's most intelligent animals. We still have a lot to learn about their behavior and routines.

Large pods often play and surf the waves around here.

SEARCH & FIND
30
ANIMALS!

MEDITERRANEAN SEA

The Mediterranean is an enclosed sea. The Strait of Gibraltar connects it to the Atlantic Ocean.

Neptune grass is an important seagrass that is vital for marine life. It lives in the Mediterranean.

You'll find it on the seabed, where it forms meadows or large underwater forests, which are home to hundreds of animals and plants.

Neptune grass looks a lot like the grass in our gardens and parks. Its green leaves gradually turn brown, and roots anchor into the ground beneath the sea.

Seagrass is extremely sensitive to environmental conditions.

Mediterranean seagrass meadows can be a good place to find species like dreamfish, sea urchins, white sea bream, and red prawns.

CHAGOS MARINE PROTECTED AREA

The Indian Ocean is the world's third largest ocean, after the Atlantic Ocean and the Pacific Ocean. It holds 20% of the world's water.

The warm climate attracts heavy monsoons, creating an environment that is home to thousands of different species. Such environmental wealth is currently endangered by pollution.

The Chagos Marine Protected Area is a great source of marine biodiversity. Lots of different kinds of puffer fish live in its deep ocean waters.

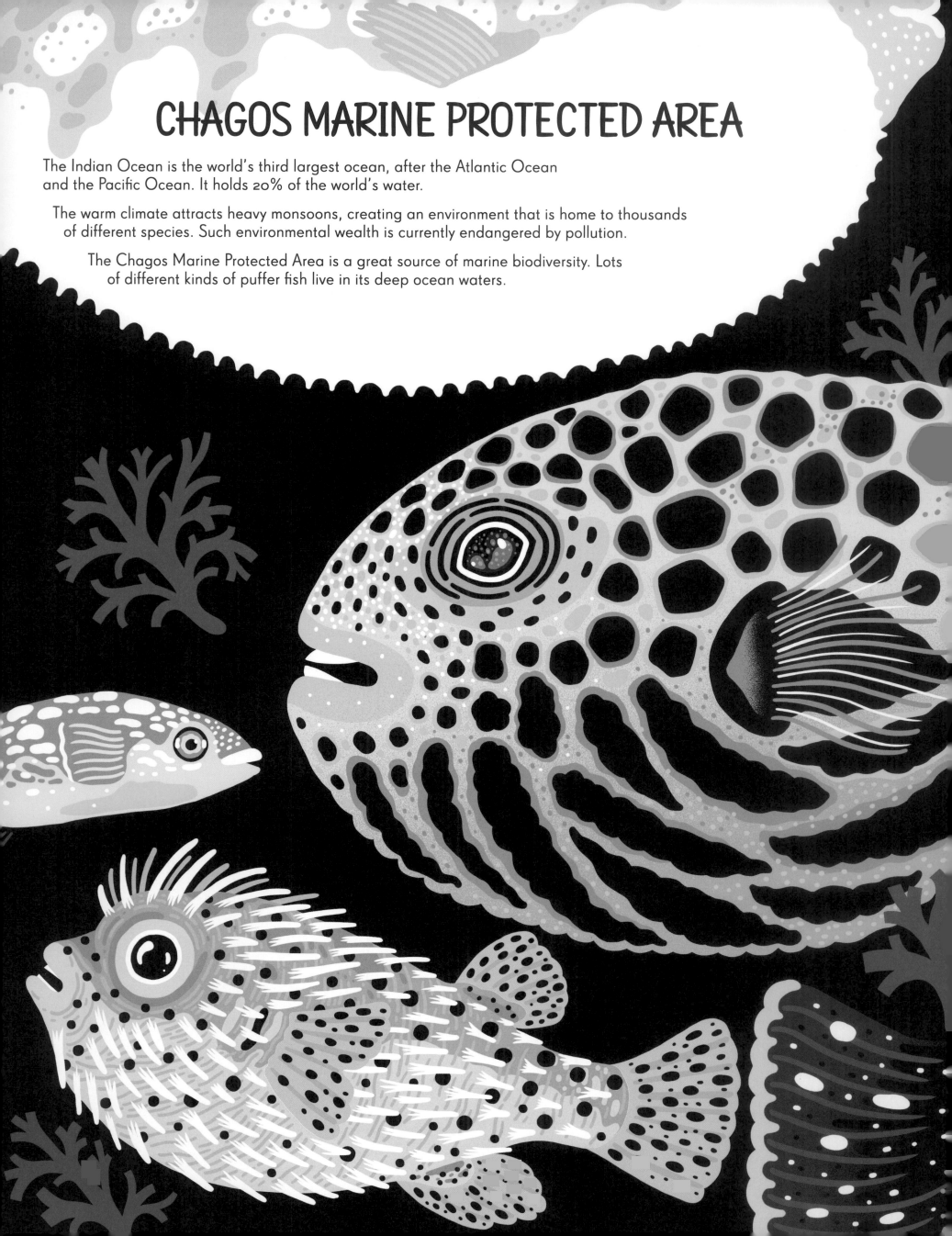

AZORES

The volcanic Azores islands belong to Portugal and are found in the North Atlantic.

Their subtropical climate is home to a wide variety of different animal species.

Sea turtles are one of their most special inhabitants. After existing for 100 million years, sea turtles are critically endangered—six out of seven species are at risk of extinction. They are all protected by law because they help keep our oceans healthy by cleaning the sea meadows, and the seabed.

SEARCH & FIND
40
ANIMALS!

FALKLAND ISLANDS

The magnificent Falkland Islands lie in the South Atlantic Ocean, more precisely in the Argentine Sea. The archipelago's subantarctic climate is very cold.

Very few people know that these island coasts are a penguin paradise. Some visitors get to witness one of the planet's most incredible migratory events.

Each year, large numbers of completely different types of penguins arrive to nest and live peacefully alongside each other.

You can see king penguins and their funny brown chicks, the Gentoo penguin or the southern rockhopper penguins with their famous yellow crest who only reach 12 inches tall.

BERMUDA

The North Atlantic Ocean is home to the legendary 181 Bermuda islands, which lie off the east coast of the United States.

Important because of their very diverse marine fauna, the archipelago is home to many of the world's most fascinating species.

Like the Flying fish—one of the most striking and peculiar animals in the sea. Their name is actually a bit misleading. Flying fish don't really fly, they glide between jumps. And although they are not very big, they can cross hundreds of yards of open water at speeds of up to 40 miles an hour!

SEARCH & FIND
2
ANIMALS!

GULF OF CALIFORNIA

The Gulf of California is an area of the Pacific Ocean separating the Baja California peninsula from mainland Mexico.

A gulf is a stretch of water that is more or less surrounded by two spikes of land. Such topography provides unique environmental features.

This gulf is one of the most diverse seas in the world. It is home to over 5,000 different marine species.

The Gulf of California is home to 37 large islands and over 300 little or tiny islands. Moving between them, you'll spot one of the loveliest marine displays: giant oceanic manta rays performing enormous leaps. Sometimes they manage to propel themselves over 6 feet out of the water.

And the funny thing is that we still don't know exactly why they do it!

SEARCH & FIND 25 ANIMALS!

ARABIAN SEA

Sitting on top of the Indian Ocean, surrounded by the Arabian coast, lies the Arabian Sea—the biggest in the world.

Its vast surface area alone isn't what makes it so big; all the earth's expanses of water are measured by their depth as well as their circumference.

This sea has four separate areas. And one of the most notorious is its abyssal zone, which is located between 13,100 and 19,700 feet below sea level. Sunlight doesn't reach these depths, so only a few species with very specific characteristics can survive in such cold conditions, where there is no vegetation and therefore very little food.

WANT TO LEARN MORE?

The number of times this creature appears on the page.

Discover more about some of these wonderful creatures.

SEA URCHINS
Sea urchins come in all shapes and sizes, and the largest in the world are the red ones. All sea urchins are pretty tough. Some are poisonous, and contrary to popular belief, the ones that have the smallest spikes are the most poisonous.

GIANT KELP FOREST

- 1 California sheep head *(Semicossyphus pulcher)*
- 2 Sea otters *(Enhydra lutris)*
- 23 Purple sea urchins *(Strongylocentrotus purpuratus)*
- 37 Red sea urchins *(Mesocentrotus franciscanus)*
- 12 Bat stars *(Patiria miniata)*
- 11 Sea snails *(Calliostoma annulatum)*
- 1 Giant sea bass *(Stereolepis gigas)*
- 1 Ocean sunfish *(Mola mola)*
- 2 Wolf eels *(Anarrhichthys ocellatus)*
- 3 Garibaldis *(Hypsypops rubicundus)*
- 2 Black rockfish *(Sebastes melanops)*
- 1 Blue rockfish *(Sebastes mystinus)*
- 2 California sea lions *(Zalophus californianus)*
- 4 California spiny lobsters *(Panulirus interruptus)*
- 12 Kelp bass *(Paralabrax clathratus)*

ARCTIC OCEAN

- 3 Orcas *(Orcinus orca)*
- 6 Walruses *(Odobenus rosmarus)*
- SHOAL Arctic cod *(Arctogadus glacialis)*
- 1 Narwhal *(Monodon monoceros)*
- 1 Beluga whale *(Delphinapterus leucas)*
- 2 Ringed seals *(Phoca hispida)*
- 6 Arctic terns *(Sterna paradisaea)*

ORCA
Scientists believe these huge predators are very intelligent. They live in families and coordinate hunting tactics by communicating between themselves. They are the largest members of the Delphinidae family, which makes them the world's largest dolphins! Some orcas weigh over 5.5 tons and measure up to 29.5 feet long.

THE GREAT BARRIER REEF

CLOWN FISH
Clownfish are amazing-looking, but their beautiful, striking colors aren't their best feature! Clownfish can be born male, but can turn female. For example if a female fish dies, her male partner changes gender to ensure the survival of the species.

SOUTHERN OCEAN

KRILL
Krill are a family of tiny crustaceans measuring around 2 inches long. There are over 90 different species of krill; it is the most abundant animal on the earth. Krill are fundamental to the world's marine ecology. They are also the main food source for whales, which can eat up to 2.2 tons of krill in one gulp. So a krill die-off would be a food chain catastrophe.

INDO-PACIFIC

FIDDLER CRABS
The fiddler crab gets its name from its oversized claw. This saltwater crustacean lives in symbiosis with coral, which means their relationship benefits them both.

COCOS ISLAND

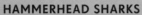

- **SHOAL** Yellowfin tuna (*Thunnus albacares*)
- **1** Indo-Pacific sailfish (*Istiophorus platypterus*)
- **14** Scalloped hammerhead sharks (*Sphyrna lewini*)
- **1** Tiger shark (*Galeocerdo cuvier*)
- **1** Hawksbill sea turtle (*Eretmochelys imbricata*)
- **3** Remora (*Echeneidae*)
- **5** Blue dragons (*Glaucus atlanticus*)
- **35** Mexican goatfish (*Mulloidichthys dentatus*)

HAMMERHEAD SHARKS
There are various species of hammerhead shark, some of which are in danger of extinction. We still don't know why their eyes are located on either side of their hammer-shaped head. Scientists and biologists have many theories, none of which have actually been proven. What we do know is that they have extraordinary peripheral vision!

CELEBES SEA

- **1** Mimic octopus (*Thaumoctopus mimicus*)
- **2** Red lionfish (*Pterois volitans*)
- **2** Yellow-lipped sea kraits (*Laticauda colubrina*)
- **3** Indonesian ocellated flounders (*Psammodiscus ocellatus*)

OCTOPUSES
Octopus are one of the oldest and smartest animals on the planet. They are very curious creatures. Interesting facts about them include that their tentacles are actually part of their brain and can continue moving even after being detached from the body. Another fact is that they have three hearts; and they squirt ink when they feel threatened!

RØST REEF

- **2** American conger eels (*Conger oceanicus*)
- **COLONY** Lophelia (*Lophelia pertusa*)
- **2** Serpent stars (*Ophiura ophiura*)
- **8** Lanternfish (*Myctophidae*)
- **COLONY** Zigzag coral (*Madrepora oculata*)
- **3** Blackbelly rosefish (*Helicolenus dactylopterus*)
- **2** Western roughies (*Hoplostethus occidentalis*)
- **3** Squat lobsters (*Eumunida picta*)

LOBSTERS
Lobsters are invertebrate arthropods. They have a very tough exoskeleton (skeleton outside their body) and five pairs of legs including a front pair that double as claws.

CAPE VERDE

- 15 Long-beaked common dolphins (*Delphinus capensis*)
- 5 Cape Verde shearwaters (*Calonectris edwardsii*)
- 1 European barracuda (*Sphyraena sphyraena*)
- 6 White seabream (*Diplodus sargus*)
- 1 Red-billed tropicbird (*Phaethon aethereus*)
- 2 Boyd's shearwaters (*Puffinus boydi*)

DOLPHINS
Dolphins are capable of understanding their environment which is why we think they are very intelligent animals. One of the most charismatic oceangoers, their complex communication skills have fascinated scientists and biologists for years.

STARFISH
Starfish aren't actually fish, they are echinoderms like sea urchins and sea cucumbers. Although most starfish have five arms, some have even more! And if any of these arms break, the starfish just grows itself another one.

MEDITERRANEAN SEA

- 1 Noble pen shell (*Pinna nobilis*)
- 9 Dreamfish (*Sarpa salpa*)
- 11 Purple sea urchins (*Paracentrotus lividus*)
- 9 Lysidice ninetta
- 6 Idotea hectica
- 4 Long-snouted seahorses (*Hippocampus guttulatus*)
- 3 Mediterranean rainbow wrasse (*Coris julis*)
- 2 Small red scorpionfish (*Scorpaena notata*)
- 1 European bass (*Dicentrarchus labrax*)
- 4 Common two-banded sea bream (*Diplodus vulgaris*)
- 1 Ornate wrasse (*Thalassoma pavo*)
- 5 Diaphorodoris papillata
- 32 Seagrass asterina (*Asterina pancerii*)
- 2 Painted combers (*Serranus scriba*)
- 8 Pygmy clingfish (*Opeatogenys gracilis*)
- 7 Red prawns (*Aristeus antennatus*)

SEAHORSES
Seahorses are one of the few species in which the male gives birth and takes care of the young. Very few baby seahorses make it into adulthood. Surprisingly, although they move their dorsal fin 35 times per second, they move very slowly and can only travel very short distances.

PUFFERFISH
Most puffer fish are poisonous. Their powerful venom is concentrated in their liver. It is one of the world's deadliest vertebrates (animals with a backbone).

CHAGOS MARINE PROTECTED AREA

- 1 Reticulated pufferfish (*Arothron reticularis*)
- 2 Milk-spotted pufferfish (*Chelonodon patoca*)
- 1 Starry pufferfish (*Arothron stellatus*)
- 1 Spiny blaasop (*Tylerius spinosissimus*)
- 1 Guineafowl puffer (*Arothron meleagris*)
- 1 Spotted porcupinefish (*Diodon hystrix*)

AZORES

- ● 2 Loggerhead sea turtles (*Caretta caretta*)
- ● 1 Sea pickle (*Pyrosoma*)
- ● 16 Pilot fish (*Naucrates ductor*)
- ● 2 Barred hogfish (*Bodianus scrofa*)
- ● 15 Moon jellyfish (*Aurelia aurita*)
- ● 1 Moray eel (*Muraenidae*)
- ● 3 Giant oceanic manta rays (*Manta birostris*)

TURTLES
Turtles can live on land or in the sea, like this one, which swims in the Indian and Pacific Oceans and is also found in the Mediterranean Sea. Young and adult turtles are extremely vulnerable in the laying season. But very few predators are capable of attacking the adults, which can weigh over 287 pounds and are protected by enormous shells.

FALKLAND ISLANDS

- ● 3 Brown skuas (*Stercorarius antarcticus*)
- ● 1 Leopard seal (*Hydrurga leptonyx*)
- ● 4 Northern rockhopper penguins (*Eudyptes moseleyi*)
- ● 9 King penguins (*Aptenodytes patagonicus*)
- ● 28 Gentoo penguins (*Pygoscelis papua*)
- ● 1 Striated caracara (*Phalcoboenus australis*)
- ● 22 Grey-headed albatrosses (*Thalassarche chrysostoma*)

PENGUINS
Penguins are birds, but their wings don't work for flying...They help make them expert swimmers. Almost every kind of penguin lives in the southern hemisphere. Evolution has gifted them with special tools to help them survive in the intense cold. For example, they have a layer of blubber under their skin to insulate their bodies.

BERMUDA

- ● 1 Tropical two-wing (*Exocoetus volitans*)
- ● 1 Mahi-mahi (*Coryphaena hippurus*)

TROPICAL TWO-WING FLYING FISH
The tropical or Blue Flying fish is found in almost every area of tropical and subtropical water on Earth, including in the Caribbean and western Mediterranean Seas. Its dark blue back contrasts with a white belly. Their wings haven't got any bones! They use them to glide through the air when they jump out of the water, which helps them travel faster.

GULF OF CALIFORNIA

🔍

- ● 20 Manta rays *(Cephalopterus manta)*
- ● 1 Giant squid *(Dosidicus gigas)*
- ● 2 Vaquitas *(Phocoena sinus)*
- ● 1 Chinese trumpetfish *(Aulostomus chinensis)*
- ● 1 Mahi-mahi *(Coryphaena hippurus)*
- ● 1 Whale shark *(Rhincodon typus)*

GIANT OCEANIC MANTA RAY
This beautiful creature has one of the biggest brains of any sea animal, making it one of earth's smartest swimmers. Manta rays can live up to 50 years and are one of the speediest creatures in the ocean. They can travel over 40 miles in a single day!

ARABIAN SEA

🔍

- ● 3 Krøyer's deep sea angler fish *(Ceratias holboelli)*
- ● 1 Goblin shark *(Mitsukurina owstoni)*
- ● 3 Cirroteuthis *(Cirroteuthis muelleri)*
- ○ 3 Silver hatchetfish *(Argyropelecus)*
- ● COLONY Boneworms *(Osedax)*
- ● 80 Mariana snailfish *(Pseudoliparis swirei)*
- ● 1 Barreleyes *(Opisthoproctidae)*
- ○ 1 Giant squid *(Architeuthis dux)*
- ● 1 Grey whale *(Eschrichtius robustus)*

ABYSSAL ZONE
The abyssal zone is the deepest and least hospitable place on earth. It is located over 13,100 feet below sea level and is too deep for the sun to reach, which means very few plants or animals can survive here. Some of the areas at these depths are unexplored by us.